SWITCHWORDS AND YOUR CHAKRAS

HOW TO USE SWITCHWORDS TO AWAKEN AND CLEAR YOUR CHAKRAS

BY

DORON ALON

Copyright information

Alon, Doron .

Switchwords And Your Chakras —1st ed

ISBN:0982472242

Printed in the United States of America

Cover image Girl With 7 Chakras © transiastock - Fotolia.com

Book Cover Design: Created by Doron Alon

doron@numinositypress.com

DEDICATION:

DEDICATED TO THE SHAKTI WITHIN

Introduction

Look around you, look at yourself. Take a good look at your hands, your feet, your thighs. Touch your hand, feel your face. All of it , everything is made and comprised of energy. A subtle Energy that we do not see with our eyes, but it is there, you can feel it, cant you? Sort of moving through you. Sometimes it doesn't feel like anything in particular, but sometimes its a buzz, or a pressure. Sometimes it's a tingling sensation throughout the body. However you experience it, there is no doubt that it's there. That, my friend, is the energy of life . Not just of your life, but of the entire universe. Everything in the universe is pulsating with this energy. In fact, science has proven that we are all made of stars. It's true, we are made of stars . What's inside of you is also spanning the entire universe. Isn't that amazing? I am in awe of it. We are , literally, a bundle of energy. A Bundle all the way down to our atoms and BEYOND.

In this book, we will cover our energy system, but also cover a simple way to clear your chakras using Switchwords. Switchwords are a somewhat obscure modality with enormous power , when combined with what can be called "Chakra tapping" it is very powerful. I will go over briefly what Switchwords are and how they work. If you want a deeper understanding of Switchwords, please take a look at my book " Switchword Miracles" In that book I go into the nitty gritty of how they work with your subconscious mind. I also cover chakras there as well, but in this book we will take it a bit deeper. With that said, let's take a quick tour of our energy system.

Chapter 1: The Energy System

As I stated in the introduction, we are comprised of energy, not only inside of us, but also outside. This energy is generally not seen with the naked eye, although some people can see it. I have only seen it once and I was astonished. I literally freaked out. I couldn't believe what I was seeing. I will get into that later**.

But before I get into the energy inside of us, let's talk a bit about the energy outside of us, the energy we can see.

Have you ever seen sunlight shine through a prism or a rainbow? The 7 main colors that emanate from the light just happen to be the same colors of our chakras and energy system. Our bodies are literally a prism in which divine light shines forth.

These colors are: Violet, Indigo, Blue, Green, Yellow, Orange and Red.

Each one of these colors has their own particular vibration and wavelength. In science these colors can be measured in NM or nanometers. Each color has its own.

Violet is the fastest frequency and shortest wavelength of the 400 NM

Indigo wave length is 445 NM

Blue wavelength 475 NM

Green is 510 NM

Yellow is 570 NM

Orange is 590 NM

Red is the longest of the wavelength clocking in at 650 NM

There are, of course, lights and colors we cannot see YET. The reason I am mentioning these things is not to teach you the intricacies of the electromagnetic spectrum. I am itemizing this to illustrate the correlation with what's outside us with the energy system inside of us. Our inner light and the light of the universe are from the same place and we share everything with it.

When you think about it, color affects everything in your life. We have strong associations with color that can produce tangible changes in the body. Some colors can sooth us, while some rile us up. Some keep us sort of blah, while others make us happy. We even use colors to describe how we feel . Have you ever "felt" Gray? Have you ever felt " RED HOT" passion? See where I am going with this? Color is everywhere and its key to understanding our Chakras. Since these colors have real influence it would be no stretch of the imagination to imagine that it also influences our chakras and energy body as well. We will get into that a bit later.

In the coming chapters, I am going to describe the various levels and types of energy that exists within us as energy beings. Knowing this will help you better visualize the process. In this chapter we will be covering Kundalini, Prana (subtle energy), Nadis or energy channels, and Meridian points. But I will focus more on the chakras over the course of the book. These energies are the fuel behind everything we experience.

Like any other system in our body, the energy system can become unbalanced. This can be due to pretty much anything. Negative thoughts, physical illness , environmental toxins, you name it. Sometimes it is often hard to tell if an imbalance caused the negative thought or the other way around. That's how intertwined it all is. But one thing is for sure, many negative experiences we have in life are due to severe energy imbalances.

Not every negative thing in life is due to a catastrophic energy imbalance; sometimes it is simply a matter of correcting a slight imbalance. Although you may experience quite dramatic negativity in your life, it could very well be a matter of a slight energy imbalance and nothing more. Do not be surprised if you experience quick relief from something you think may be too large for you to handle. Again, for legal purposes I can't make any guarantees, all I can tell you is that if you give this book an honest attempt, I feel you will gain a lot from it. You don't have to believe any of this in order for it to work, that's the beauty of it. Often we are told that you must believe in something in order for it to work. Well, if that's the case, many people are going to have a hard time changing anything.

Ok, let's talk about the energy system as a whole and then drill deeper into the chakras.

Kundalini and Prana

The energy that is flowing through the chakras is called Kundalini. Since this energy is mostly feminine in nature, another name used for it is Shakti; Shakti is the embodiment of feminine energy in the universe. The word Kundalini means "Coiled", it is called this because the common imagery used to illustrate this energy is as a snake coiled up at the base of the spine or the root chakra. When you start engaging the chakras, this energy slowly unravels and works its way up the body. There are many reported physical sensations when the kundalini unfolds. It is for this reason it is imperative that you " get clear" before activating this energy. The person who is not prepared could risk experiencing some adverse side effects of engaging the Kundalini directly. Its prevalent enough that they even have a term for it. Kundalini Syndrome. These symptoms can range from fairly benign tingling in the hands to trembling and in some cases far worse. Some have suggested that many mental disorders may be due to spontaneous awakening of

Kundalini. Deep emotional states can trigger the awakening as well. So it is wise to always be responsible and take things slow when you work with it.

Prana is a different energy, but it is interrelated. Prana is defined in Sanskrit as "life force" the "Elan Vital" as it were. Prana is largely responsible for our physically functioning, it's all regulated subconsciously. This energy travels throughout a network of pathways in our bodies called Nadis or Meridians. It's a tad difficult to describe this energy because the force itself is intangible and "ethereal" in nature.

In order to explain both Prana and Kundalini let us try to relate the two. Prana, as I mentioned is responsible for much of our psychophysical needs. In this way, kundalini is almost identical to Prana; however, Kundalini has a far wider reach than Prana. Pranic energy work is simply a stepping stone to Kundalini work. This is important to know because in the west, many people practice Kundalini yoga thinking they are doing a good thing but in fact they are causing much more damage to themselves. If they have Pranic blocks, awakening Kundalini can be quite a negative experience as I stated earlier. It is like trying to force yourself to lift very heavy weight without building up to it. Serious injury can ensue from that endeavor. Switchwords and Chakra tapping together help release the blocks in the Chakras which will allow us to work on them. Often, after a few sessions, the Chakras will immediately self regulate once the blockage is gone. Trust me, you'll know when that occurs. It is for this reason you will find that during the exercises, I will do an initial chakras tapping sequence to get clear. Getting clear is essential in order to release any energetic blocks you might have.

Nadis and Meridian Points

Nadi in Sanskrit means river or channel; there are many Nadi points in the body. These points are located on the physical body as well as throughout the energetic system. They are used to transport energetic substances in and out of our bodies, both subtle and physical.

They are, in essence, channels for the life force aka Prana. In Chinese acupuncture, nadis are referred to as meridian points. Our quality of life depends on the ease of which energy flows throughout these points. In order to remain healthy in both mind and body, the nadis/meridian points must be cleared as well. Not unlike our bodies, any blockages in our energy can mean the difference between life and death. If there are any blockages, they can cause untold misery in your life both physically and mentally. Since these points are throughout the body, any blockage in any of them inevitably causes physical ailments as well. The Nadis that are in the energy system are channels for our many thoughts and feelings both positive and negative. When the energy is blocked, we grow complacent with life. We isolate from others and can often fall into deep depression. These blocks also cause us to make decisions that we would not make if we were clear. I should know, I was one big energetic block. My life was in turmoil because of it ...So I speak from experience. I ate too much, weighed too much, drank too much and ruined a perfectly wonderful relationship.

It's safe to say that my energy was chaotic and several blockages were present.

The chakras that we will cover later in this book play a very important role in how our entire energy system is regulated. Since the Nadis are conduits of energy, they are very important for the energy flows in and out of our chakras and elsewhere in the body. Since these Nadis and Meridian points are vast in number, its impossible to cover them in one book. First we will do a quick Nadi cleanse and then we will use Switchwords and Chakra tapping together to unblock any blockages you may have. Once we clear out the main energetic arteries we can let the full energetic potential of our lives express itself and flow. These energies are so powerful, often, once they are cleared, it immediately reprograms and overrides the subconscious mind. It can literally undo years of trauma. This clearing will also allow you to clearly work towards your goals. The first step is to clear those energy pathways. Since this book is predominately about the chakra system, that's what we will focus on the most, but I will do at least one Nadi/Meridian cleanse. If you would like to

learn how to clear out the Meridians points in more detail,

please refer to Switchword Miracles for more tapping routines.

**Side note: As I mentioned earlier, I had one encounter when I actually saw my own Prana. I was out with a friend who happens to be a very talented psychic. She asked me if I ever did something called a "Prana Ball". I never heard of it. She said" Hold your hands in a way that appears like you are holding a ball". I did so, after a while I could feel the heat between my two hands increase. During this time, my eyes were closed. After about 2 minutes of having my eyes close, I open them. I couldn't believe it. My hands were glowing. NO JOKE. This white-gold colored light, just a bit under half an inch was extending out of my hands. It didn't move, it was static, my hands were simply glowing. I tried to touch it, but you can't really, it's just a glow, It's like trying to touch the light coming out of a light bulb. It's just there. I couldn't believe what I was seeing. I have seen Prana in my mind, but never physically. It was quiet an eye opening experience for me. I have no doubt Prana is real...I saw it with my own eyes.

Chapter 2: The Wheels of Life

Chakra clearing and chakra work have almost become clichés in the self-help and new age circles. You will find countless yoga instructors using chakra meditations . There are countless books on the chakra system, some quite scholarly and some that seem , well, a bit alien. I am going to cut through some of the fat and give you a brief but clear understanding of the chakras and what they signify.

The word Chakra comes from the Sanskrit word *cakram,* which means wheel. In Hindu art they are often depicted as flowers with a set number of petals. These flower petals are interconnected in such a way that they appear as spokes in a wheel, they are visualized as whirling wheels of energy situated along the spine in what is called the "Subtle Body". The subtle body is in essence an energetic double of ourselves. This double is not fully outside of us, but intertwined with our physical body. Due to this intertwining with the body, energy flowing through the subtle body affects everything in the physical body as I stated earlier. These Chakra energy centers are moving clockwise and are the main avenue for the reception and transmission of energy both physically and spiritually.

The whole concept of the Chakra system has been gleaned from ancient Hindu texts. Some of these texts may be the oldest text in existence. There are 7 chakra centers in our bodies, some traditions say that we have more, but for our purposes we will deal with the more common view that we have 7 chakras. However, as an added bonus I will mention a few other "lower" chakras as well just to give you an idea of what is out there.

In the illustration below you will see where the various chakras are. I will give a description of each one here.

Girl With 7 Chakras © transiastock - Fotolia.com

The Root Chakra

Our first chakra is known as the root Chakra. In Sanskrit this chakra is known as Muladhara. The root chakra is our foundational chakra and can be found at the very end of our spine and right atop the genitals.

The color associated with this chakra is red. Red can be a vital and living color but can also be associated with anger and frustration. Since this a foundational chakra the element that it most closely resonates is with earth. We are firmly rooted in Earth whether we want to be or not. This chakra, when balanced, will keep us grounded.

In general, chakras not only affect us spiritually but can also affect our bodies as I mentioned early. Since this chakra is at our lower extremities, it will influence those regions.

This chakra has a profound influence on the digestive system, especially the lower digestive system as well as the kidneys and adrenal glands. If you have issues with any of these areas, it may be partially due to a block in this chakra. A block often manifests in sluggishness, fatigue, constipation. It is responsible for insomnia, lower back pain , eating issues on both spectrums. Emotionally, an imbalance will often lead to depression, instability, irritability and anger, addiction and irrational fearfulness.

If all is well in this chakra, you feel secure, grounded, your body functions properly and waste is efficiently released from your body. Often a balanced Root is also associated with financial wellbeing . Without money in this world, you cannot be secure. A balanced root chakra will be very helpful here.

Seed Sound for this Chakra: Lam. **(We will be incorporating these seed syllables in our chakra clearings.)**
Color: Red.
Switchwords: ADJUST, ALONE,BE,CHARLTON HESTON, CHARM,CHLORINE,CHUCKLE,CIRCULATE,CLASSIC,CLEAR,CONFESS,CONSIDER, CONTINUE, COPY,COUNT, COVER, CRISP,CROWD,CRYSTAL, CUT,DEDICATE, DIVINE ORDER,DONE,DUCK,FIFTY THREE, FIGHT, FIND,FORGIVE, FULL,GIVE, GO, GUARD,HALFWAY,HO,HOLD, HOLE,HORSE,HORSE SHOE, JACK LALANNE,LEARN,LIMIT,LOVE,MAGNANIMITY, MASK,MONA LISA,MOVE, NOW, OFF, OFFER, OIL,ON,OPEN,OVER,PERSONAL,

PHASE, POSTPONE,PRAISE,PUT, REJOICE, RESCIND,
RESTORE,REVERSE, RIDICULOUS,ROOT,SAVE,SCHEME,
SHOW,SHUT,SOPHISTICATE, SPEND,STRETCH, SUFFER,SWIVEL,
TAKE,TAP,TOGETHER, UNCLE,UP,WASTE, WOMB.

As an aside, most of the issues that I had in my life were due to a severe imbalance in my root chakra. I had pretty much everything that was associated with it.

Some say that you can see the color of the aura and chakras with a special form of Photography called "Kirlian photography". Well, I tried it twice, over the span of 2 days with two different photographers and my entire aura was red, a deep blood red. When I saw that, I knew that I needed to clear that up. My root chakra was clearly tumultuous.

As an added bonus I will also include the names of what some say are the "lower chakras" meaning they are lower on the body than the Root Chakra. The 7 chakras below are considered the drivers of our baser animal instincts.

Atala: This one governs our sense of fear and our lustful energy. It is located at the hips.

Vitala: This governs our resentments and anger and is located in the thigh area.

Sutala: This one drives jealousy and is located at the knees.

Talatala: When imbalanced causes confusion and is located in the calves.

Rasatala: This the center of our selfishness and is located at our ankles.

Mahatala: Located at our feet and is associated with spiritual and conscious darkness

Patala: This is located at the soles of our feet and houses our hatred and malice towards others and life.

I will not get into those, but I thought it would be interesting to know.

The Sacral Chakra

The Sacral chakra is our second one. In Sanskrit is called Swadhisthana. This chakra is located in and around the lower abdomen; approximately 2 inches below the navel. The color associated with this chakra is Orange.

This chakra is an "emotional" one. It has a profound influence on them. And like emotions, this chakras element is water. The body location of this chakra most closely influences the ovaries and testicular regions of the body. Similar to the root chakra, this one can also influence the kidneys and stomach, in addition to the pancreas, spleen, gallbladder and liver.

As you may have guessed, this chakra influences our sexuality, our general emotional states, our interpersonal relationships and our own acceptance of ourselves.

If this chakra is out of balance, several physical and emotional issues may arise. Such as , low libido , impotence, lower back pain, hormonal imbalances, urinary tract infections, fatigue and generalized pain in the lower extremities. Emotionally, one may experience excessive need for control and perfectionism. Increased irritability, excessive shyness (I am still working on this), enhanced states of guilt and shame that can lead to addiction. if you ever feel stifled creativity, this too can be an imbalance in this chakra.

If this chakra is balanced, it can be quite beautiful. You can experience increased sexuality and the ability to expertise true intimacy and take pleasure in the things that you do. Your relationships will be harmonious and without drama. A balanced Second chakra essentially imparts a joy for life.

On a personal note, this chakra was also stifled in me. When I meditated some years ago I was trying to help dissipate the build of energy in my root chakra and as I visualized the red hot energy move up, it looked like it almost completely bypassed the second chakra. The second chakra was dull and almost lifeless, at least that is how the initial visualization came to me. This should have been no surprise, I was experiencing little to no sex drive, I isolated myself from others and it was just not a good time for me. Interestingly enough, all that changed when I came across switchwords.

Seed Sound: VAM

Element: Water

Color: Orange.

Switchwords:

ADJUST,BE,BUBBLE,CANCEL,CANCER,CHANGE,CHARLTON HESTON,CHARM,CHLORINE,CHUCKLE,CIRCULATE,CLASSIC,CON FESS,CONSIDER,

CONTINUE,COPY,COUNT,COVER,CRISP,CRYSTAL,

CUT,DEDICATE,DIVINE ORDER,DONE,DUCK,ELATE,FIGHT,FOR,FULL,GIVE,GO,HALFWAY ,HELP, HO, HOLD,HOLE,HORSE,HORSE SHOE, JACK LALANNE,LEARN,LIGHT,

LOVE,MASK,MOVE,NOW,OIL,OPEN,OVER,PERSONAL,PHASE,P OSTPONE, PRAISE, PUT,REJOICE,RESCIND,RIDICULOUS,

ROOT,POSTPONE,SHOW, SOPHISTICATE, SPEND, STRETCH,

SUFFER, TAKE,TAP,THANKS,TINY,TOGETHER, TOMORROW,

UNCLE, UP,WITH,WOMB.

The Solar Plexus Chakra

The third chakra is the solar plexus chakra. Its located between the bottom of your rib cage and your navel. I tend to visualize right at or above the navel area. This chakras name is Manipura and its color is yellow. This chakra represents our thinking mind and our ability to take action in life.

 The physical area this charka governs are similar to the previous chakra; kidneys ,the gallbladder, liver, pancreas, spleen and also the mid-spine region and part of the little intestine. The major gland however is the pancreas.

If this chakra is out of balance , you may experience the following emotional issues. Low and very low self worth and esteem. Body image issues, but also your general image of yourself. This chakra, is imbalanced may also stifle your desire to take action and cause you to be timid about things.

If this chakra is not balanced you may experience physical issues such as bulimia or anorexia, liver issues, colon issues. Ulcers, pancreas issues as well as arthritis.

If the chakra is balanced, the opposite of the above would be true. Your mind will be clear, you will have healthy self worth , strong positive desire for life and a strong sense of self. Not to mention, your organs will work more efficiently, especially your pancreas which will help your blood sugar. When blood sugar is stabilized your mental and physical states are also stabilized and you won't feel or experience wild swings in mood, energy or appetite for that matter.

Seed Sound: RAM

Element: Fire

Color: Yellow.

Switchwords: BE, BUBBLE, CANCEL, CANCER, CHANGE, CHARM,CHLORINE, CHUCKLE, CIRCULATE, CLASSIC, CONFESS, CONTINUE, COUNT, COVER, CRISP, CRYSTAL, CUT, DEDICATE, DIVINE ORDER, DO, DONE, ELATE, FIGHT, FOR, FULL, GIVE, HALFWAY, HELP,HO, HOLD, HORSE, HORSE SHOE, JACK LALANNE, LEARN,LOVE, MASK, MOVE, NOW, OIL, ON, OPEN, OVER, PERSONAL, PHRASE, POSTPONE, PUT, REJOICE,

RESCIND, RESTORE, RIDICULOUS, ROOT, SAVE, SCHEME, SHOW, SOPHISTICATE, SPEND, STRETCH, SUFFER, SWEET, SWING, TAKE, TAP, THANKS, TINY, TOGETHER, TOMORROW, UNCLE, UP,WITH, WOMB.

The Heart Chakra

The fourth chakra or Heart Chakra called Anāhata in Sanskrit Is situated in the center of the chest just right of the heart area itself.

The heart, throughout all human history has always been associated as the seat of love and sometimes seat of the soul. It is a major chakra and is often at the center of the chakras since it distills the lower chakras energies so it may move up and relaxes the energy from the higher chakras when traveling down to the lower chakras.

The color that is most associated with this chakra is green but sometimes pink.

Aside from the heart itself, this chakra also governs the arms, hands, shoulders, the lungs, breasts and the entire circulatory system.

When this chakra is out of balance it can wreak havoc on the emotions. Deep feeling of despair may be experienced where hope doesn't exist. If you find it too difficult to open up and love can also be a symptom of an imbalance in this chakra. Like the root chakra, this imbalance can lead to anger, hatred and fear.

When this chakra is out of balance it can lead to heart problems, various pulmonary diseases of which asthma is a part of. Pain the shoulders, arms. May even cause breast cancer, but also growths of a noncancerous type as well.

A balanced heart chakra, often appears as a sense of nurturing, optimism, compassion and feelings of wholeness with oneself. But also connectedness to others and the ability to love another. Often this chakra is hurt more often than others because of life events. Heartbreak, grief etc can really throw this chakra out of balance.

Seed Sound: YAM

Element: Air

Color: Green sometimes pink

Switchwords: ALONE, BE, BUBBLE,CANCEL,CHANGE,CHARM,CHLROINE, CHUCKLE, CIRCULATE,CLASSIC, CONFESS,CRISP, CRYSTAL, DEDICATE, DIVINE ORDER, FULL,GIVE, HO,HOLD,HORSE,HORSE SHOE, LEARN,LOVE, MASK, MOVE,OIL, OPEN, PERSONAL, POSTPONE, PUT, REJOICE,RESCIND, RIDICULOUS,ROOT, SHOW,

SOPHISTICATE, STRETCH, SUFFER,SWEET, TAKE, TAP, THANKS, TINY,TOGETHER,TOMORROW, UNCLE, UP,WITH,WOMB.

The Throat Chakra

The fifth chakra or Throat Chakra called Viśuddha in Sanskrit Is situated in the throat area itself. This chakras color is blue. This chakra is the chakra of communication and expression. Since it is located at the throat, the corresponding organ to this chakra is the thyroid. This tiny organ regulate our metabolism and if it is imbalanced can cause either unhealthy weight loss or weight gain. It also has a role in memory, energy levels or lack thereof. This chakra is also center around the vocal cords, the neck and nearby areas.

If the throat chakra is not balanced, this can seriously influence your creativity, your ability to express yourself verbally. Often people with imbalanced throat chakra find it hard to speak up and this builds up and often these people develop thyroid problems. On the other extreme, it can also display itself as a lack of control when it comes to speech. So the person with an imbalanced chakra may speak too much. it can work both ways. Other manifestations of this imbalance involve dishonesty and being overly harsh and critical and on the flip side, under spoken or too soft spoken for our own good.

As I stated earlier, the thyroid tends to be the one hit hardest by an imbalanced throat chakra. The second most common illness associated with an imbalanced chakra are throat issues in general. I know of a person who stifles her emotions and has had a hard time speaking up for herself. It manifested by frequent bouts of strep throat, tonsillitis, ear infections and related issues. Although she does not know about the chakras, one thing is for certain, when she took back her power, interestingly enough, her throat issues went away. She did connect her throat issues with her communication issues but not in terms of it being a chakra issue. In either case, the results are quite dramatic. She even started to get in shape because she no longer had negative communication with her own psyche.

When this chakra is balanced, communication flows easily, your creativity is sparked and the ease to which it flows is very noticeable. When this chakra is balanced, you are able to create boundaries with people and have the ability to speak your mind. Self awareness also becomes easier since your inner communication channels are not blocked.

Seed Sound: HAM

Element: Sound

Color: Blue

Switchwords: ACT, ATTENTION, BOW, CHARM, CONCEDE, COUNT, CRYSTAL, CURVE, CUT, CUTE, DIVINE ORDER, DOWN, ELATE, FOREVER, FORGIVE, FULL, GIGGLE, GIVE, HO, HOLD,HORSE,HORSE SHOE ,LEARN, LIGHT,LIMIT,LOVE, MAGNANIMITY, MASK, MONA LISA, MOVE, OPEN, PERSONAL, POSTPONE, PRAISE, PUT, REJOICE, RESCIND, RESTORE, REVERSE, RIDICULOUS, ROOT, SHOW, SOPHISTICATE, STRETCH, SUFFER,SWEET,TAKE, TAP, THANKS, TINY, TOGETHER, TOMORROW, UNCLE, UP, WITH, WOMB.

The Third Eye Chakra or Brow Chakra

The sixth chakra or Brow Chakra called Ājñā in Sanskrit Is situated right between the eyes. This is by far the most popular of the chakras, most people have heard of the third eye and for good reason. This is the eye of discernment and wisdom, your mind's eye if you will. This chakra is represented by the beautiful color of indigo.

The gland that this chakra most connects to is the pituitary gland. This gland regulates many aspects of the body including how tall you will be, your skin coloring and various aspects of childbirth. It is often called the master gland because it has a profound effect on all the other glands and hormones in your body. Since the 3rd eye is positioned right between the eyes, the brain , eyes and nose are also within its jurisdiction so to speak.

If this chakra is not balanced it can be devastating. Often an imbalanced third eye has been associated with ADHD, certain mental illnesses that cause disassociation with reality. Judgment in general can be impaired leading to confusion and "brain fog".

Physically, the imbalance can show in alarming ways. Often severally imbalanced 3rd eye can lead to panic attacks, brain tumors, migraine headaches, various learning disabilities, strokes and other ischemic attacks, as well as severe nightmares and the like.

if this chakra is balanced, we gain tremendous physical and mental benefits. Our intuition will be heightened, our ability to manifest our thoughts for good is also more apparent. Our concentration will be laser-like. It can open a completely new world for you. Both the inner and outer world.

Seed Sound: OM

Element: Light

Color: Indigo

Switchwords: ADD, AROUND, BETWEEN,BLUFF, BRING, BUBBLE,

CANCEL,CANCER,CARE,CHARM,CLIMB,CRYSTAL,CUTE,DIVINE,

DIVINE ORDER, DOWN,ELATE,FULL,GIGGLE,GIVE,

HELP,HO,HOLD,HORSE, HORSE SHOE, JUDGE,LEARN,

LISTEN,LOVE,MASK,MOVE,NEXT,

OIL,ON,OPEN,PERSONAL,POINT,POSTPONE,PUT,QUIET,REACH,

RESCIND, ROOT,SAGE,SHOW, SOPHISTICATE,

STRETCH,SUFFER,TAKE,

TAP,TOGETHER,UNCLE,UNMASK,UP,WAIT,WATCH,

WHET,WOMB.

The Crown Chakra

The seventh chakra or Crown Chakra called Sahasrāra in Sanskrit Is situated right at the top of the head. This chakra serves as your spiritual gateway. It is also the location where life/divine energy enters into the chakra system and your body. It is no coincidence that in almost every religion, gods, prophets and holy people all had light shine from the tops of their heads in the form of halos. That shine is from a developed Crown Chakra. An imbalance in the Crown Chakra can cause self centeredness, but a special form of self centeredness called Spiritual narcissism. Spiritual narcissism develops when a person has such a strong sense of spirituality that instead of channeling that for the benefit of others it translates into feelings of superiority. This is very pervasive in the self help community. An imbalance at this chakra can also lead to some astounding delusions. When this chakra is developed we experience deep understanding, spiritual connection and bliss. This level has no concern for duality. It has transcended both time and space. When balanced, we become more selfless, more connected to the divine and more loving towards all of existence. This chakra , like the third eye also over sees the brain and many of the same symptoms of imbalance are presented.

Seed Sound: Deep silence

Element: Cosmic energy

Color: Violet

Switchwords: BRING, CARE, CHARM, CLIMB, CRYSTAL, DIVINE, DIVINE LIGHT, DIVINE ORDER, FULL, GIVE, HO, HOLD, HORSE, HORSE SHOE, LEARN, LISTEN, LOVE, MASK, MOVE, OPEN, PERSONAL, POSTPONE, PUT, QUIET, RESCIND, ROOT, SHOW, SOPHISTICATE, STRETCH, SUFFER, TAKE, TAP, TOGETHER, UNCLE, UNMASK, UP,WAIT, WOMB.

As you can see, the chakra system is very important for our wellbeing and must be tended to as we would tend our overall health. In the next chapter we will discuss Switchwords and what they are. After that, we will put it all together.

Chapter 3: Switchwords

We are now entering the meat of this book. Switchwords are the star of the show. In this chapter, I will be going into a bit of detail regarding Switchwords. I will provide a comprehensive list of all the main Switchwords and which chakra they are tied to at the end of the chapter .

I stumbled upon Switchwords by "accident". I was going through a breakup and I have to say, it was a really really dark moment in my life. It was my fault, I had negative emotional habits that caused me to become overly sensitive, which in turn caused me to stagnant in life . This brought out a lot of anger and insecurity. Unfortunately, there are emotional consequences to being in that state. Consequences that inevitably led to losing a woman I loved so much. In fact, she is "the girl that got away". This was a bitterly painful time. I forgot what exact search term I was using on Google, but somehow I was guided to Switchwords. I have read hundreds if not thousands of books in the self help and spiritual genres and thought I had pretty much seen it all. Nothing new and innovative was coming out and despite having a brain full of transformative tools, I felt dead inside.

I was very frustrated because I wasn't able to get the results I wanted and it was certainly not for lack of trying. Something was missing and I needed a boost and I needed it fast. It got so bad that I recall being stone drunk on Easter Sunday, crying and throwing my books away and ripping some of them to shreds. Something that I later regretted. It was BOTTOM for me. It was at that low point when Switchwords appeared. I have never heard of them before and doing a search I could see that it wasn't showing up like the other methods that saturate the internet with millions of search results. Put in "law of attraction" (with the quotation marks to focus the search results) and you get as of the time of this writing, 73,800,000, that is over seventy three million results, It's everywhere. Now put in "Switchwords" and you get 41,900. This number was much lower when I wrote my first book on the topic" switchword miracles" . 41,900 is a very low number in terms of search results. I felt that I was on to something, something that few people knew about. I researched them further and I am glad I did. I am a different person today because of them and now I am bringing them to you, so you too can be transformed.

What are Switchwords and how were they discovered?

Switchwords were discovered by a colorful man by the name of James T. Mangan. In his book "The Secret of Perfect Living" he states that the subconscious mind has several "switches". When these switches are flipped, they can produce certain outcomes. Shunyam Nirav has also contributed greatly to the understanding of Switchwords. He is the author of "Switchwords Easily Give to You Whatever You Want in Life" . These switches are certain words or a combinations of words. In many ways they are one-word affirmations or a string of one word affirmations. Unlike sentences, or affirmations like "I am wonderful just as I am " they don't make sense in the conventional sense. The conventional affirmations contain statements that your subconscious does not believe is true (that's why they generally do not work as I stated in Switchword Miracles). Switchwords , however, bypass the "interpretive" aspect of your mind and engage the subconscious mind directly, thus making the result automatic. This is vital because if your communications with the subconscious mind are drawn out like affirmations, you are giving the subconscious mind the opportunity to cancel those affirmation and dig in, thus making change harder. With Switchwords, it is a switch, there is no opportunity for the subconscious mind to block or interpret it. It simply switches the state on. Sometimes it requires a few repetitions, but it works. I swear by it. If you do research you won't find many people saying negative things about them. You may ask, 'If Switchwords are so powerful, why combine them with Chakra work and tapping?" You can use both modalities separately if you like. However, they are enhanced when used together.

Some have asked me 'If Switchwords are so effective, why haven't I heard of them?" I asked the same question. I have come to realize they are not as popular because they simply aren't attractive and flashy like the other kinds of modalities. They can't be packaged with flowery language and you can't really create countless elaborate exercises. They are simple and paired down.

Sorry for the diversion, now back to the origin and elaboration of Switchwords. James Mangan identified approximately 100 Switchwords that are extremely effective when used with a specific goal in mind. Others have added to the list as well. The beauty of using Switchwords is that you don't need to believe it will work in order for it to. It's like gravity, you can say it doesn't exist until you are blue in the face but it will work on you regardless of whether you believe in it or not. This is another reason why Switchwords are more effective than traditional affirmations. There is no belief involved. I know I am sounding like a broken record here but it is very important to keep this in mind. With conventional affirmation you are told to believe the affirmation is true. I don't know about you, but it was VERY hard for me to believe that " I am perfect as I am and I have unlimited money in the bank". As I mentioned earlier, the subconscious will kick that idea out and may even entrench the opposite of that affirmation even deeper. In this way, conventional affirmations can be dangerous because it may make your current situation worse because the subconscious mind wants to entrench it deeper after being exposed to the conventional affirmation that it knows to be false. It is no wonder why so many people seem to get worse after using the Law of Attraction in the conventional way. They are fighting an entrenched force the wrong way... in this case, less is more my friend.

In essence, Switchwords capture the core and energy of a desired result or experience. There is no right or wrong way to use them, you can sing them, declare them, chant them or say them in the quiet of your own mind, that's how I do it. Say them once or thousands of times a day, whatever way you feel will create results for you. Just remember that more is not always better. Sometimes just mentioning them once a day will work just fine. No matter how you use them, they work and you really can't go wrong.

Here are a few examples of how you can use Switchwords:

Let's say you want to get in the mood to write, you can simply say the Switchword "GIGGLE" either once or several times and you will notice that you will start getting in the mood to write.

Let's say you lost something, you can use the Switchword " REACH" and it will guide you in the right direction. REACH can also be used to retrieve a memory or "reach" for a new idea or solution to a problem.

I often use the Switchwords " UP" and "MOVE" when I need extra energy and within a few minutes that energy comes to me. In fact I use the Switchwords ," UP-MOVE- HALFWAY" when I run and it really helps right away. I wouldn't be able to run like I do without saying those 3 words. I also say UP-MOVE when I wake up. It works.

I will now provide you with a comprehensive list of Switchwords and their respective uses. The list below contains "Universal or Master Switchwords" that James mentions in his book. Many of the Switchwords can be used interchangeably so you may find one word feels better to use than another for your particular situation. You will also notice that many Switchwords can be used for several different situations. I will also specify which chakra those words resonate with the most. Many have overlap and some connection you may see that I did not. In general, however, this list should be pretty accurate.

Universal / Master Switchwords and how they can help you:

ACT: If you would like to become a good speaker. **(Thoat Chakra)**

ADD: This is to increase what you have, no matter what it is. **(Third Eye Chakra)**

ADJUST: This is a great one to create balance in your life. It will also help you handle uncomfortable or unpleasant conditions. **(Sacral Chakra) (Root Chakra)**

ALONE: This will help you nurture or heal yourself or another. This will help you increase focus on yourself but not in a self absorbed way but in terms of nurturing and healing yourself. **(Root Chakra) (Heart Chakra)**

AROUND: This will help you gain or improve your perspective. **(Third eye Chakra)**

ATTENTION: This will help you do detailed work and avoid carelessness. This will apply to other areas of your life as well, not only work. **(Throat Chakra)**

BE: This is a powerful one, this will help you to achieve peace and good health. it will help you have good form; dispel loneliness; increase your skill in sports. it also has the added benefit of helping you brush off ridicule from others. **(Root, Sacral, Solar Plexus, Heart Chakras)**

BETWEEN: This one is often used to develop intuition and psychic abilities. It works. **(Third Eye Chakra)**

BLUFF: This one is good to get rid of nervousness or fear as well as increase your imagination. It is especially good to use when you want to create pleasant dreams. **(Third Eye Chakra)**

BOW: This helps reduce any arrogant tendencies you may have. **(Throat Chakra)**

BRING: This is a manifestation Switchword, it helps you unite with your goal, helps you finish what you started. **(Third eye, Crown Chakra)**

BUBBLE: This Switchword is really good at helping you expand your perceived limits, it is also good for creating a mood of excitement and energy. **(Third eye, Sacral, Solar Plexus and Heart Chakras)**

CANCEL: Use this Switchword to eliminate negative thoughts and conditions. It helps eliminate debt, poverty and other unwanted conditions. Which in turn will dispel worry. I use this one when I feel insecure about something. **(Third eye, Sacral, Solar Plexus and Heart Chakras)**

CANCER: To clarify, this does not mean cancer the disease but rather the zodiac sign. This Switchword is used to calm emotional distress and to soften outlook. **(Third eye, Sacral, Solar Plexus)**

CARE: This one is used to help you retain or memorize anything you need to remember or retain. You can say it before you read something so as to remember it. **(Third Eye, Crown Chakra)**

CHANGE: This helps get rid of emotional and physical pain. It also helps get something out of the eye.**(Sacral, Solar Plexus and Heart Chakras)**

CHARLTON HESTON: I admit, I feel silly saying this one sometimes but it is good to keep you mindful about your posture. Helps you stand straight and tall. You can use someone elses names who stands straight or tall with confidence. **(Root and Sacral Chakras)**

CHARM: This will help you manifest your heart's desire. **(All Chakras)**

CHLORINE: This will help you mingle and share yourself with others. Helps you make a difference; blend in and become one with. **(Root, Sacral, Solar Plexus, Heart Chakras)**

CHUCKLE: This one helps you turn on personality. **(Root, Sacral, Solar Plexus, Heart Chakras**

CIRCULATE: This helps you end loneliness and helps you feel at ease so you can mingle with people. **(Root, Sacral, Solar Plexus, Heart Chakras)**

CLASSIC: Use this one to appear cultured and suave . **(Root, Sacral, Solar Plexus, Heart Chakras)**

CLEAR: This one will help you dispel anger and resentment you may towards yourself or others.**(Root Chakra)**

CLIMB: This will help you enhance your view point, rise above it all. **(Third eye, Crown Chakras)**

CONCEDE: This helps to reconcile and end arguments between people. You can use it if you want to be at peace with someone. **(Throat Chakra)**

CONFESS: This ends aggression very well. **(Root, Sacral, Solar Plexus, Heart Chakras)**

CONSIDER: This helps you become more handy . use it before fixing your car or putting together a piece of future etc. **(Root Chakra, Sacral Chakra)**

CONTINUE: This helps create or increase endurance for both physical and mental tasks. **(Root, Sacral, Solar Plexus Chakras)**

COPY: this helps you have good taste and also increases fertility. **(Root and Sacral Chakras)**

COUNT: This will help you make money and help you reduce or stop smoking **(Root, Sacral, Solar Plexus and Throat Chakras)**

COVER: reduce nervousness; subdue inner excitement **(Root, Sacral, Solar Plexus Chakras)**

CRISP: This is a great one to dispel fatigue, feel refreshed, revitalizes. It also helps brighten your mood. **(Root, Sacral, Solar Plexus, Heart Chakras)**

CROWD: This helps reduce or eliminate disobedience in children, pets or subordinates at work. **(Root Chakra)**

CRYSTAL: This is a powerful Switchword that will help you clarify any situation or things. It helps you look to the future; both mentally and through clairvoyance. This can help you access Universal Knowledge. I use this one to clarify intentions when I feel blocked. **(All Chakras)**

CURVE: This helps to create beauty; make something beautiful. This is good to enhance creativity.**(Throat Chakra)**

CUT: This will help you achieve moderation in all your actions. it can also help you make proactive decisions regarding toxic relationships. Essentially giving you the strength to sever ties with a toxic person if you have to. **(Root, Sacral, Solar Plexus and Throat Chakras)**

CUTE: This will help you think; discern; be sharp-witted and be clever. **(Third Eye and Throat Chakras)**

DEDICATE: This will help you to stop clinging to either a person or a situation. **(Root, Sacral, Solar Plexus and Heart Chakras)**

DIVINE: This one will help you work miracles or accomplish extraordinary things, it increases personal ability. **(Crown Chakra and Third Eye Chakras)**

DIVINE LIGHT: This will help you focus on positivity, multiply intensity of any thought; increase spiritual enlightenment. **(Crown Chakra)**

Divine Order: This will help you with any organizing or cleaning you need to do. It helps you be more efficient making sure things are in optimum order. I use this when I feel disorganized with my thoughts or do not know where to start something. It helps bring order. **(All Chakras)**

DO: eliminate procrastination in its tracks with this one. **(Solar Plexus)**

DONE: This is a great one against procrastination as well . it helps you meet a deadline or keep a resolution. It's great for building willpower . **(Root, Sacral, Solar Plexus Chakras)**

DOWN: This helps you become more humble. People don't like braggarts , this will help eliminate that trait in you if bragging is a problem for you. **(Third eye and throat Chakras)**

DUCK: This helps dispel sensitivity about looks or capabilities. Helps you shrug off criticism. **(Root , Sacral Chakras)**

ELATE: This helps transform a setback into a positive uplifting event. **(Third Eye, Throat, Heart, Solar Plexus, Sacral Chakras)**

FIFTY THREE (53): This helps you take primary responsibility over something. **(Root Chakra)**

FIGHT: This helps you win a competitive game and intensify your efforts and intentions. **(Root, Sacral and Solar Plexus Chakras)**

FIND: This helps you build a fortune and can be used with Switchword "COUNT". **(Root Chakra)**

FOR: This will help you promote anything. **(Sacral and Solar Plexus Chakras)**

FOREVER: This will help you keep a secret .**(Throat Chakra)**

FORGIVE: This will help you cool your anger and end desire for revenge . This also helps dispel   remorse. **(Root and Throat Chakras)**

FULL: This help you achieve optimum levels to help you go beyond and expand your capacity in any endeavor. **(All Chakras)**

GIGGLE: This will get you in the mood for writing. It will also help you enjoy the task at hand. **(Third Eye and Throat Chakras)**

GIVE: To sell something and to help others. **(All Chakras)**

GO: This will help you end laziness. Helps you begin and progress in anything. I use it when I feel like I don't want to start something right away. I say GO and I get motivated. **(Root, Sacral Chakras)**

GUARD: This help protect you from bodily hard, spirit or your property. it helps to preserve your personal safety. **(Root)**

HALFWAY: This helps make a long distance seem short. This is one of 3 Switchwords I use to make my long runs easier. it also helps me better handle projects that require long tedious work. **(Root, Sacral, Solar Plexus)**

HELP: This helps eliminate indecision or uncertainty and increases focus. **(Third eye, Solar Plexus, Sacral Chakras)**

HO: Saying this one helps you relax and reduce tension. **(All Chakras)**

HOLD: This helps to build character. **(All Chakras)**

HOLE: This will help create attractiveness and sex appeal in yourself. **(Root, Sacral Chakras)**

HORSE: This will help you be solid, strong and gain personal power . **(All Chakras)**

HORSESHOE: This will help you remain steadfast and strengthen the soul during times of challenge. It will help you safely move rapidly ahead and remain sturdy throughout. **(All Chakras)**

JACK LALANNE: this will help you be enthusiastic (or you use someone you know who is an enthusiast about something) **(Root, Sacral and Solax Plexus Chakras)**

JUDGE: This will help you love reading and increase your comprehension of what you read. I use this all the time when I read. **(Third Eye Chakra)**

LEARN: act and be youthful; rejuvenate your mind and soul. **(All Chakras)**

LIGHT: This will help you be inspired, lighten load or mood. It's a great stress reducer. **(Throat Chakra, Sacral Chakras)**

LIMIT: set parameters, regain control. This will help keep others from taking advantage of you.**(Throat and Root Chakras)**

LISTEN: This will help you predict the future. This is also very powerful when you want to get in touch with nature and yourself. **(Crown and Third Eye Chakras)**

LOVE: This will help generate, radiate and experience love of all types. **(All Chakras)**

MAGNANIMITY: This will help you eliminate pettiness and increase generosity. **(Root and Throat Chakras)**

MASK: Protect and shield from harm . **(All Chakras)**

MONA LISA: This will help bring a smile to your face and dispel hatred and envy. (Or you can use someone who represents a smile to you) **(Root and Throat Chakras)**

MOVE: This is great to increase energy and eliminate tiredness. It is one of the 3 words I use every time I run, without fail. (**Solar Plexus, but can really be used for all chakras as well.)**

NEXT: This will help you finish lots of meticulous work and be able to endure more. (**Third Eye)**

NOW: This ends procrastination. It also helps you to act on good impulses. (**Root, Sacral, Solar Plexus Chakras)**

OFF: This one is used quit an unwanted habit AND it helps you go to sleep. This Switchword does help me sleep. If I wake up in the middle of the night, I can rely on "OFF" to help me get back to sleep quickly. I love it. (**Root Chakra)**

OFFER: This will help dispel greed. (**Root Chakra)**

OIL: This will help external and internal friction. Smooth and release tensions and resistance. (**Third eye, Heart, Solar Plexus, Sacral and Root)**

ON: This is a very powerful Switchword to help you get new ideas; obtain transportation; nourish your ambition. (**Third Eye, Solar Plexus, Root)**

OPEN: This will he help you inhibitions. It will increase tolerance and understanding. it can free the mind and allow feeling and ideas to flow easily. **(All Chakras)**

OVER: This will help end frustration. (**Solar Plexus, Sacral and Root Chakras)**

PERSONAL: This will help you be a success. it will help you publish a successful newspaper or newsletter or book for that matter. **(All Chakras)**

PHASE: This will help you set goals. Set a routine or pattern and improve your situation. **(Solar Plexus, Sacral and Root Chakras)**

POINT: This will improve eyesight and focus. It will help you find direction and make a clear decision. **(Third Eye)**

POSTPONE: This helps you to let things go. **(All Chakras)**

PRAISE: This will help you be beautiful or handsome and will help you to stop being overly critical with yourself. **(Throat, Sacral and Root Chakras)**

PUT: This will help you build and expand. You can use this for any endeavor you want to build or expand. **(All Chakras)**

QUIET: This will help quiet the ego. If you feel you must get the last word in, say QUIET and you will notice how that urge will subside. I used this the other day and I was able to just let it all go and let the other person have their moment. **(Crown and Third Eye Chakras)**

REACH: This is great to locate misplaced objects and reach solutions for problems. It will help you repair things. It will help you recall forgotten ideas and information in your mind or memory like names, numbers etc. I used this twice and it worked very well. i am not one to lose my keys, in fact, I NEVER DO. When I did, I used this Switchword and I found it very quickly and in the most unlikely place. The fridge. (I have no idea how they got in there). **(Third Eye)**

REJOICE: When you encounter someone who is more successful in something that you want success in, it is easy to feel jealous. This Switchword will help dispel jealousy. **(Throat, Heart, Solar Plexus, Sacral and Root Chakras)**

RESCIND: This will help you undo; restart; cancel; redo; something. Some other teachers of Switchwords recommend that this switchword should Always be used with the Switchwords; BETWEEN, CRYSTAL and LISTEN in order to avoid as they say "possible time loop." I can't say I know exactly what that means, but erring on the side of caution can't hurt. **(All chakras)**

RESTORE: This will help restore fairness and honesty . **(Throat, Solar Plexus, Root Chakras)**

REVERSE: This will help you get rid of grudges or stop a repetitive pattern in the moment. **(Throat and Root Chakras)**

RIDICULOUS: This will help you gain a lot of attention. **(Throat, Heart, Solar Plexus, Sacral and Root Chakras)**

ROOT: This will help you discover and grow in any area of your life. **(All Chakras)**

SAGE: To help you dispel evil in the mind or your home. **(Third Eye)**

SAVE: This will help you stop drinking alcohol and other unwanted habits. I used this word with POSTPONE to help me when I was drinking a lot. **(Root, Sacral and Solar Plexus Chakras)**

SCHEME: This is great for those of you who want to advertise, design and create marketing plans or PR for your company or business. **(Solar Plexus, Root Chakras)**

SHOW: This will help you raise your moral standards and help you develop respect for people and yourself. **(All Chakras)**

SHUT: When you feel a bit reckless and sad, use this to help you stop looking for trouble. **(Root Chakra)**

SOPHISTICATE: This will help you publish a successful magazine or book. It will also help you become a great success . **(All Chakras)**

SPEND: This will help you develop a sense of style. **(Solar Plexus, Sacral and Root chakras)**

STRETCH: This will will help you prolong a good feeling ,event or a sense of well-being you are experiencing. It will also help you grow intellectually, spiritually and physically. By grow I mean become better. **(All Chakras)**

SUFFER: This will help you handle success and prosperity . Often we think that once we are successful that it will be easy. Often times it is not, with great success comes great responsibility. This Switchword will help you handle it. I sure could have used this word 10 years ago. **(All Chakras)**

SWEET: This will help you be soothing and caring to others. **(Throat, heart and Solar Plexus Chakras)**

SWING: This will raise your courage and boldness. **(Solar Plexus)**

SWIVEL: relieve constipation and diarrhea. All I am going to say about this one is that...it works. **(Root Chakra)**

TAKE: This will help you become a good leader . This is great for people who find that they need to develop leadership skills quickly. **(All Chakras)**

TAP: This will help you convert; adapt; renovate anything. **(All Chakras)**

THANKS: This will help increase gratitude in your heart and will help release guilt. **(Throat, Heart, Solar Plexus and Sacral)**

TINY: This will help you be polite , kind hearted and courteous. It will also you decrease the importance of something that bothers you. Some have said this helps with weight loss as well. **(Throat, Heart, Solar Plexus and Sacral)**.

TOGETHER: This is considered to be THE Master Switchword to help you master any activity. Get things all together. It is also used to become single-minded when you need to be. I will mention this one again in the section on how to create Switchwords for yourself. It's the most powerful Switchword in the list. **(All Chakras)**

TOMORROW: This will help you eliminate remorse and sorrow . **(Throat, Heart, Solar Plexus and Sacral)**.

UNCLE: dispel un-togetherness and separateness. **(All Chakras)**

UNMASK: This Switchword will help bring things into focus; expose; lay bare before you. **(Crown and Third Eye Chakras)**

UP: This will help elevate your mood and help you defeat feelings of inferiority. (**All Chakras)**

WAIT: Saying this will create a situation where you will learn a

secret. (**Crown and Third Eye Chakras)**

WASTE: This will help you appear rich and show opulence . (

Root Chakra)

WATCH: This will help you learn a skill or perfect a skill you

already have. (**Third Eye)**

WHET: This one will help stimulate, sharpen and refine anything

you put your mind upon. (**Third Eye)**

WITH: This will help you be agreeable and compatible with

others. (**Throat, Heart, Solar Plexus and Sacral Chakras)**

WOMB: This will help you attract and feel cuddled and safe.

This will help you reconnect with Divinity and mother nature.

(Crown And Root Chakras, essentially all of them)

Chapter 4: Putting It All Together

In this chapter we will be putting the various pieces together into a practice.

As I stated earlier in the book, aside from the chakras, we have other energy path ways called meridians. These are channels that feed in and out of the chakras. They spread the energies throughout the body. If any of them are blocked they can inhibit the flow of chakra energy throughout the body. So for our first exercise, we will clear out those meridians so the chakra energies can flow through them. The way we do this is through something called EFT or Meridian tapping. If you read my first book " Switchword Miracles" you know I am a big fan of the process. If you haven't read it, I will explain the gist of it here.

Since Meridian points are essentially acupuncture points, it has been proven that by tapping those points with our index and middle fingers as opposed to putting a needle in them often produces the same results. So for this exercise we will be tapping on a few points in order to clear them. Below you will see a diagram of the points we will be tapping.

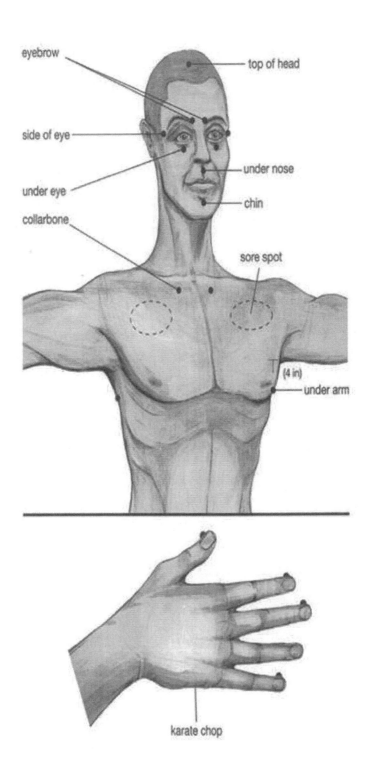

Sorry, it isn't the best picture in the world, but it serves our purposes. So each point that is labeled will be tapped. You only need to tape each point 3-4 times. While we tap we will be making certain statements on each point. These statements serve to help focus our intentions as we clear out the various meridian points.

The tapping circuit starts with tapping the karate chop point, then the eye brow point, side of the eye, under the eye, under the nose, the chin, the sore point or collar bone point as it is also called, then under the arms and then top of the head. The circuit will not take more than a minute or so, if not less. I will guide you through the tapping session below.

Tapping Session # 1: Our intention for this tapping session will be to unblock any energy from flowing between the meridian points and the chakras.

Take a deep breath and repeat after me:

Karate chop point: Although my energy system make have blockages, I chose to accept myself anyway.

Eyebrow point: I intend to clear any and all blockages that exist between my meridian points.

Side of the Eye: I intend to clear out any and all blockages between my chakras and my meridian points.

Under the Eye: I intend to clear out any and all blockages between my chakras.

Under the Nose: Why is it that my energy system is working so well?

Chin point: Why is it that my chakras are well balanced?

Sore point aka Collar bone point: I know that with an harmonious meridian and chakra system, my life will get better.

Under arm point: My desire is strong for healthy and vibrant chakras

Top of Head: I realize that my meridian points are now clear and so it is.

Take a deep breath. You may already feel a cleansing of the energy system. Often people report that a single tapping session or at most two are all they need. However, for the purposes of this book, we will be taking it a bit deeper.

Tapping Session 2: Now we will awaken each chakra individually using its respective seed syllable. For this exercise we will be tapping on the various body parts that correspond to the various chakras. The tapping can be gentle it does not have to be a hard tap.

Where to tap:

Root chakra: We have 2 options, since the first option may not be comfortable for everyone. One way to tap the root chakra is tap lightly right above the genital area. If you are uncomfortable doing so, you can tap the very base of your spine on your back.

Sacral Chakra: The tapping point for this one is about 2 inches below the belly button.

Solar Plexus: The tapping point for this one is right at or slightly above the belly button.

Heart Chakra: The tapping point for this one is right in the middle of the chest between the breast.

Throat Chakra: The tapping point for this one is right at the throat where the Adams apple is located.

Third Eye Chakra: The tapping point is right at the middle of the forehead.

Crown Chakra: The tapping point for this one is at the crown of the head.

In this sessions we will take each point 2-3 times while stating the seed syllable and visualizing the corresponding colors associated with the chakras.

The steps:

Tap the Root Chakra: Visualize the color red and chant LAM 3 times.

Tap the Sacral Chakra: Visualize the color orange and chant VAN 3 times.

Tap the Solar Plexus Chakra: Visualize the color yellow and chant RAM 3 times.

Tap the Heart Chakra: Visualize the color Green and chant YAM 3 times.

Tap the Throat Chakra: Visualize the color blue and chant HAM 3 times.

Tap the Third Eye Chakra: Visualize the color Indigo and chant OM 3 times.

Tap the Crown Chakra: Visualize the color violet and sit in silence for a few second.

Take a deep breath and relax for a minute or two. You have just stirred the chakras awake.

Tapping session 3: Embedding the power of Switchwords into your Chakras.

Now that your chakras are awakened and cleansing themselves, we will not embed the Switchwords power into them. Since this first series of taps is to clear the chakras in a general way, we will use switchwords most conducive for this purpose. After this session, I will do more targeting tapping sessions so you get the gist on how to use it for various situations in your life. For this example I will pick 2 switchwords and use them together as a "Switchphrase" but you are welcome to use only one word. I am going to pick Switchwords **Together and Crystal.** These 2 together are very useful for clearing. You may also visualize the chakras colors as you do the exercise below, but it is not necessary.

The steps:

Tap the Root Chakra: And say _Together-Crystal_ 3 times.

Tap the Sacral Chakra: And say _Together-Crystal_ 3 times.

Tap the Solar Plexus Chakra: And say _Together-Crystal_ 3 times.

Tap the Heart Chakra: And say _Together-Crystal_ 3 times.

Tap the Throat Chakra: And say _Together-Crystal_ 3 times.

Tap the Third Eye Chakra: And say _Together-Crystal_ 3 times.

Tap the Crown Chakra: And say _Together-Crystal_ 3 times.

Take a nice deep breath. That's really all there is to it. You should feel the energy start flowing steadily through you. You are welcome to do this as many times as you want. Often I hear that 2 times on any given day is enough. I personally do this once when I wake up. Sometimes I will do a few more based on a particular part of my life that I need clarity on.   Which will not lead me to the next chapter. I will show you how to apply the above technique to certain areas of your life. You will see that these techniques can be used for any issue.

Chapter 5: Targeted Chakra Work

In this chapter I will show you how to apply the above tapping routines to specific areas of your life. In order to do this, we will not be focusing on the enter chakra system as we did in the last chapter, but specific chakras. So you will find 14 sessions, 2 for each chakra and a corresponding issue.

The first 7 issues we will deal with are : Financial debt, Relationships, Self worth and self esteem, lack of forgiveness/holding on to trauma, not being able to communicate what you want, excessive worrying, depression.

The second 7 issues we will deal with health problems specific to those chakras such as : Joint pain, sexual issues, diabetes, high blood pressure, thyroid problems, headaches, nervous system disorders. This, of course, is not an exhaustive list of physical issues, there are other issues that correspond to each chakra. I am simply stating these as an example, you can adapt all of this to suit your particular needs.

As a legal disclaimer, I am not able to make any guarantees that these techniques will work for you. Your best bet is try them out yourself and see how they work for you. Consult a professional before trying to remedy any issues you may have.

The first 7: Financial debt, Relationships, Self worth and self esteem, lack of forgiveness/holding on to trauma, not being able to communicate what you want, excessive worrying, depression.

Like in the previous chapter, we will start with a meridian tapping session. However, we will follow that with a Chakra session but only using one chakra and a switchword session only using one chakra as well.

1. Financial Lack: Root Chakra.

Tapping Session 1: Meridian Tapping Sessions

Karate Chop Point: Although I have this crushing debt, I am open and willing to love myself anyway.

Eye Brow Point: I see this debt in front of me and I am willing to get rid of it.

Side of Eye Point: This debt has no room in my life anymore.

Under Eye Point: I am willing to do what it takes to get rid of this debt.

Under Nose Point: I choose to live debt free life from now on.

Chin Point: I realize this debt will be resolved.

Collar Bone Point: I release this debt once and for all.

Under Arm point: This debt has overstayed its welcome.

Top of head point: I intend to be debt free for the rest of my life. Take a deep breath, now one to Tapping sessions 2, the chakra tap.

Tapping Session 2: The Chakra Tap

Tap the Root Chakra: Visualize the color red and chant LAM 10 times.

Take a deep breath.

Tapping session 3: Embedding the power of Switchwords into your Chakras.

For this sessions I will choose the 2 main Switchwords for financial abundance. **FIND - COUNT.**

Tap the Root Chakra: And say _FIND COUNT_ 10 times.

That concludes the session for financial debt. You can do this as many times as you like. This will awaken your root chakra which is the chakra that when out of balance can cause us to experience financial issues.

2. Relationships: Sacral Chakra.

Karate Chop Point: Although I feel closed off to love, I am open and willing to love myself anyway.

Eye Brow Point: I am willing to conquer this fear of intimacy issue I have once and for all.

Side of Eye Point: I am willing to let go of this fear of intimacy and start living .

Under Eye Point: I am willing to do what it takes to reduce my fear of intimacy.

Under Nose Point: I intend to love again.

Chin Point: I realize this fear of intimacy can be resolved.

Collar Bone Point: I choose to release any anxiety I have about relationships.

Under Arm point: This loneliness has overstayed its welcome.

Top of head point: I intend to embrace love and intimacy with courage.

Tapping Session 2: The Chakra Tap

Tap the Sacral Chakra: Visualize the color orange and chant VAN 10 times.

Take a deep breath.

Tapping session 3: Embedding the power of Switchwords into your Chakras.

For this sessions I will choose the main Switchword to become open in relationships . **OPEN.**

Tap the Sacral Chakra: And say _OPEN_ 10 times.

That concludes the session for relationships. You can do this as many times as you like. This will awaken your sacral chakra which is the chakra that when out of balance, can cause us to experience intimacy issues.

3. Self Worth And Self Esteem : Solar Plexus Chakra

Karate Chop Point: Although I have low self esteem and self worth, I am open and willing to love myself anyway.

Eye Brow Point: I feel this crushing low self esteem and I am willing to let it go TODAY.

Side of Eye Point: These feeling of low self worth has no room in my life anymore.

Under Eye Point: I am willing to do what it takes to get rid of this awful helpless feeling.

Under Nose Point: I choose to live in a state of self worth.

Chin Point: I realize these negative feeling will go away.

Collar Bone Point: I release these helpless feeling once and for all.

Under Arm point: This feeling of self worth has overstayed its welcome.

Top of head point: This helplessness will be gone.

Tapping Session 2: The Chakra Tap

Tap the Solar Plexus Chakra: Visualize the color yellow and chant RAM 3 times.

Take a deep breath.

Tapping session 3: Embedding the power of Switchwords into your Chakras.

For this sessions I will choose the main Switchword to become more confident and steadfast in self esteem . **CRYSTAL-HORSE.**

Tap the Solar Plexus Chakra: And say _CRYSTAL-HORSE_ 10 times.

That concludes the session for self esteem and self worth. You can do this as many times as you like. This will awaken your solar Plexus chakra which is the chakra that when out of balance, can cause us to feel as if we have lost our personal power.

4. Forgivness/Holding on to Trauma: Heart Plexus Chakra

Karate Chop Point: Although I have a hard time forgiving the person/persons who have hurt me, I choose to love and accept myself anyway.

Eye Brow Point: I feel this trauma in my mind and body and I am ready to let it go.

Side of Eye Point: it might be hard to forgive, but I am willing to give it a chance

Under Eye Point: I feel that the person who inflicted this trauma in me will always haunt me in my mind.

Under Nose Point: I feel like the cause of my trauma will be around forever, but I know it won't.

Chin Point: I realize these negative feeling can and will go away.

Collar Bone Point: I release these the source of my trauma and I am willing to forgive.

Under Arm point: This feeling of bitterness has overstayed its welcome.

Top of head point: Trauma be gone.

Tapping Session 2: The Chakra Tap

Tap the Heart Chakra: Visualize the color Green and chant YAM 10 times.

Take a deep breath.

Tapping session 3: Embedding the power of Switchwords into your Chakras.

For this sessions I will choose the main Switchwords to heal trauma pain and allow you to forgive . **BE-CHANGE.**

Tap the Heart Chakra: And say _BE-CHANGE_ 10 times.

That concludes the session for Forgiveness and trauma. You can do this as many times as you like. This will awaken your Heart chakra which is the chakra that when out of balance, can cause us to feel as if we have lost our personal power.

5. Not being able to communicate what you want - Throat Chakra

Karate Chop Point: Although I have a hard time expressing myself, I intend to accept myself anyway.

Eye Brow Point: I feel stifled and unheard and I am willing to let that go today.

Side of Eye Point: I wont allow anyone to muffle my voice any more.

Under Eye Point: I will be impeccable with my word from now on.

Under Nose Point: I will speak up for myself and not allow anyone to shut me up.

Chin Point: I will be honest with myself and others starting NOW.

Collar Bone Point: I will allow myself freedom of expression.

Under Arm point: This feeling of being stifled has outlived its time with me

Top of head point: I will be heard

Tapping Session 2: The Chakra Tap

Tap the Throat Chakra: Visualize the color blue and chant HAM 10 times.

Take a deep breath.

Tapping session 3: Embedding the power of Switchwords into your Chakras.

For this sessions I will choose the main Switchwords to heal your communication issues . **ACT-HORSE.**

Tap the Throat Chakra: And say _ACT-HORSE_ 10 tImes.

That concludes the session for Communication. You can do this as many times as you like. This will awaken your Throat Chakra which is the chakra that when out of balance, can cause us to feel stifled and not heard.

6. Excessive Worrying - Third Eye Chakra

Karate Chop Point: Although I worry myself sick, I intend to accept myself anyway.

Eye Brow Point: I need to stop worrying so much.

Side of Eye Point: I wont allow anyone or thing to worry me.

Under Eye Point: I intend to live a worry free life.

Under Nose Point: I know worrying is useless and I am willing to let it go.

Chin Point: I can see that most of my worry is groundless.

Collar Bone Point: I will stop worrying and making others worry.

Under Arm point: This feeling of worry is eating away at me and I have had enough.

Top of head point: Worry? Who?

Tapping Session 2: The Chakra Tap

Tap the Third Eye Chakra: Visualize the color Indigo and chant OM 10 times.

Take a deep breath.

Tapping session 3: Embedding the power of Switchwords into your Chakras.

For this sessions I will choose the main Switchwords to heal your worry . **CANCEL-BUBBLE.**

Tap the Third eye Chakra: And say _CANCEL-BUBBLE_ 10 times.

That concludes the session for WORRY. You can do this as many times as you like. This will awaken your Third eye Chakra which is the chakra that when out of balance, can cause us to feel excessive worry.

7. Depression - Crown Chakra

Karate Chop Point: Although I feel depression and or anxiety I chose to love and forgive myself anyway.

Eye Brow Point: I feel that I can start living a happy life TODAY.

Side of Eye Point: my depression and anxiety has no room in my life.

Under Eye Point: Depression and anxiety will be gone.

Under Nose Point: I choose to remedy my depression and anxiety in a healthy way.

Chin Point: I realize that depression can go away.

Collar Bone Point: I release this depression and anxiety.

Under Arm point: depression be gone

Top of head point: Anxiety, take a hike.

Tapping Session 2: The Chakra Tap

Tap the Crown Chakra: Visualize the color violent and sit in silence for a few seconds.

Take a deep breath.

Tapping session 3: Embedding the power of Switchwords into your Chakras.

For this sessions I will choose the main Switchwords to heal your depression . **TOGETHER-BUBBLE-UP.**

Tap the Crown Chakra: And say *TOGETHER-BUBBLE-UP* 10 times.

That concludes the session for depression. You can do this as many times as you like. This will awaken your Crown Chakra which is the chakra that when out of balance, can cause us to feel depressed.

You can use any Switchword you want from the Switchword list for these exercises. I simply used the most obvious ones to me. You should experiment and see which one works for your purposes best. You can also recite the switchwords and Seed syllables more than 10 times. I have simply used 10 times because that is what I do. Feel free to adapt it.

The second 7 issues will deal with health problems specific to those chakras such as : Joint pain, sexual issues, diabetes, high blood pressure, thyroid problems, headaches, nervous system disorders. This, of course, is not an exhaustive list of physical issues, there are other issues that correspond to each chakra. I am simply stating these as an example, you can adapt all of this to suit your particular needs.

1. Joint Pain: Root Chakra.

Tapping Session 1: Meridian Tapping Sessions

Karate Chop Point: Although I have this joint pain, I am open and willing to love myself anyway.

Eye Brow Point: I release any and all psychological reasons for this joint pain.

Side of Eye Point: I release all physiological reasons for this joint pain.

Under Eye Point: I am willing to understand the pain in order to let it go.

Under Nose Point: I choose to live pain free.

Chin Point: I realize this pain won't be forever

Collar Bone Point: How would my life be without pain?

Under Arm point: I allow pain to go away for good.

Top of head point: Pain be gone.

Tapping Session 2: The Chakra Tap

Tap the Root Chakra: Visualize the color red and chant LAM 10 times.

Take a deep breath.

Tapping session 3: Embedding the power of Switchwords into your Chakras.

For this sessions I will choose the 2 main Switchwords for Pain. **TOGETHER- CHANGE.**

Tap the Root Chakra: And say _TOGETHER-CHANGE_ 10 times.

That concludes the session for joint pain. You can do this as many times as you like.

2. Sexual issues: Sacral Chakra.

Karate Chop Point: Although I have this sexual issues _____ I am willing to accept myself anyway.

Eye Brow Point: I am willing to overcome any resistance I have to solving my issue.

Side of Eye Point: I intend to have a healthy sex life .

Under Eye Point: I am willing to overcome any sexual dysfunction I may have.

Under Nose Point: I intend to learn the reason why I have this issue.

Chin Point: I realize this fear of intimacy can be resolved.

Collar Bone Point: I choose to release any anxiety I have about sex.

Under Arm point: This sexual issue of_____ has overstayed its welcome.

Top of head point: I intend to embrace love and intimacy with courage.

Tapping Session 2: The Chakra Tap

Tap the Sacral Chakra: Visualize the color orange and chant VAN 10 times.

Take a deep breath.

Tapping session 3: Embedding the power of Switchwords into your Chakras.

For this sessions I will choose the main Switchword to help with sexual issues . **TOGETHER-OPEN-STRETCH.**

Tap the Sacral Chakra: And say <u>TOGETHER-*OPEN-STRETCH*</u> 10 times.

That concludes the session for sexual issues. You can do this as

many times as you like.

3. Diabetes : Solar Plexus Chakra

Karate Chop Point: Although I have diabetes I am willing to love my body anyway

Eye Brow Point: Even though my blood sugar is not completely balanced, I am willing to listen as to why.

Side of Eye Point: How would it feel if I did not have diabetes anymore?

Under Eye Point: I am willing to give myself a chance to get rid of this condition.

Under Nose Point: I choose to live in a state of vibrant health.

Chin Point: I realize these things happen for a reason and I am willing to find out why.

Collar Bone Point: I release these helpless feeling about diabetes once and for all.

Under Arm point: Diabetes has overstayed its welcome.

Top of head point: Pancreas, become whole!

Tapping Session 2: The Chakra Tap

Tap the Solar Plexus Chakra: Visualize the color yellow and chant RAM 3 times.

Take a deep breath.

Tapping session 3: Embedding the power of Switchwords into your Chakras.

For this sessions I will choose the main Switchword for diabetes. **TOGETHER-BE-FULL.**

Tap the Solar Plexus Chakra: And say _TOGETHER-BE-FULL_ 10 times.

I hat concludes the session for self esteem and self worth. You

can do this as many times as you like.

4. High Blood Pressure: Heart Plexus Chakra

Karate Chop Point: Although I have high blood pressure, I am willing to let it go.

Eye Brow Point: My doctor said I have high blood pressure. I will do what I can to remedy it.

Side of Eye Point: I intend to lower my blood pressure in healthy ways.

Under Eye Point: I see myself healthy again

Under Nose Point: I feel like the cause of my high blood pressure will be around forever, but I know it won't.

Chin Point: I realize high blood pressure can be controlled and I tend to find out how.

Collar Bone Point: I release the cause of my high blood pressure.

Under Arm point: This high blood pressure has overstayed its welcome.

Top of head point: My heart is healed and whole.

Tapping Session 2: The Chakra Tap

Tap the Heart Chakra: Visualize the color Green and chant YAM 10 times.

Take a deep breath.

Tapping session 3: Embedding the power of Switchwords into your Chakras.

For this sessions I will choose the main Switchwords to heal trauma pain and allow you to forgive . **TOGETHER-BE-CHANGE-HO.**

Tap the Heart Chakra: And say TOGETHER-*BE-CHANGE-HO* 10 times.

That concludes the session for high blood pressure. You can do this as many times as you like. Just the tapping itself alone can reduce your blood pressure.

5. Thyroid Problems - Throat Chakra

Karate Chop Point: Although I have issues with my thyroid, I am choosing to love myself anyway.

Eye Brow Point: I am going to understand why I have these thyroid issues.

Side of Eye Point: I won't allow my thyroid issues to stop me from living.

Under Eye Point: I will do what it takes to rid myself from my thyroid issues.

Under Nose Point: I will balance out my throat chakra so my thyroid will work better.

Chin Point: I will be free of this issue.

Collar Bone Point: I will allow myself freedom to let go of these thyroid problem.

Under Arm point: This feeling a bit scared about my thyroid issue, but I know I will be okay.

Top of head point: Thyroid issues be gone.

Tapping Session 2: The Chakra Tap

Tap the Throat Chakra: Visualize the color blue and chant HAM 10 times.

Take a deep breath.

Tapping session 3: Embedding the power of Switchwords into your Chakras.

For this sessions I will choose the main Switchwords to heal your thyroid. **BE-CHANGE-CLEAR.**

Tap the Throat Chakra: And say _BE-CHANGE-CLEAR_ 10 times.

That concludes the session for thyroid issues. You can do this as many times as you like.

6. Headaches - Third Eye Chakra

Karate Chop Point: Although I have this throbbing head, I choose to love myself anyway.

Eye Brow Point: I wish this headache would go away.

Side of Eye Point: I am open to learn the reason why I have these headaches.

Under Eye Point: I intend to live headache free.

Under Nose Point: I know headaches can go away and I tend to find out how to get rid of them.

Chin Point: I see myself being rid of my head aches forever.

Collar Bone Point: I give up holding on to the reasons why my head hurts..

Under Arm point: Headaches are not for me

Top of head point: Headaches? What headaches?

Tapping Session 2: The Chakra Tap

Tap the Third Eye Chakra: Visualize the color Indigo and chant OM 10 times.

Take a deep breath.

Tapping session 3: Embedding the power of Switchwords into your Chakras.

For this sessions I will choose the main Switchwords to heal headaches . **TOGETHER- CHANGE.**

Tap the Third eye Chakra: And say _TOGETHER-CHANGE_ 10 times.

That concludes the session for headaches. You can do this as many times as you like.

7. Nervous System Disorders - Crown Chakra

Karate Chop Point: Although this nervous system disorder_____ I choose to love myself anyway.

Eye Brow Point: I feel that despite my illness I can live a full life.

Side of Eye Point: my nervous system disorder _____ will not get the better of me.

Under Eye Point: I choose to find a way to rid myself of this issue.

Under Nose Point: I choose to remedy it as soon as possible.

Chin Point: I realize that this disorder is here for a reason and I will find out why.

Collar Bone Point: I release this now.

Under Arm point: Nervous system disorder _____ be gone

Top of head point: I will regain my health.

Tapping Session 2: The Chakra Tap

Tap the Crown Chakra: Visualize the color violent and sit in silence for a few seconds.

Take a deep breath.

Tapping session 3: Embedding the power of Switchwords into your Chakras.

For this sessions I will choose the main Switchwords to heal a nervous disorder. **TOGETHER-DIVINE-CHANGE-BE.**

Tap the Crown Chakra: And say _TOGETHER-DIVINE-CHANGE-BE_ 10 times.

That concludes the session for Nervous system disorder. You can do this as many times as you like.

You can use any Switchword you want from the Switchword list for these exercises. I simply used the most obvious ones to me. You should experiment and see which one works for your purposes best. You can also recite the switchwords and Seed syllables more than 10 times. I have simply used 10 times because that is what I do. Feel free to adapt it.

Power Tip 1: To add more power to the Switchword portion of the session you can add the switchword **Together** to the other switchwords. It enhances the power of the other switchwords used.

Power Tip 2: If you would like to create your own switchwords. Simply have your intention in mind and recite TOGETHER 10 times and whatever word comes to mind is your own switchwords for your own purposes. Isn't that neat?

Conclusion

There you have it. I am hoping you have enjoyed reading this book as much as I enjoyed writing it. Switchwords, as you can see, can be used in so many ways. It's for this reason I have written several books on the topic. Every book showing a different way switchwords can be used. Apply what you have learned here on a regular basis and I feel confident you will experience the shifts that you need. You can experiment and use different Switchwords for different chakras and see how it works for you. Nothing in this book is set in stone. Like all modalities, sometimes it requires some adaptation and personal tailoring to fit it into your life.

Thanks again for allowing me to share this with you. I hope it brings you joy. If you have any comments or just want to say hi, please feel free to email me below.

Namaste,

Doron

doron@switchwordmiracles.com

DISCLAIMER

As a legal disclaimer, I am not able to make any guarantees that these techniques in this book will work for you. Your best bet is try them out yourself and see how they work for you. Consult a professional before trying to remedy any issues you may have.

About The Author

Doron Alon is a bestselling author of 50 books, in 3 different genres and is founder of Numinosity Press Inc.

He writes on a wide variety of topics including History, Self-help, Self-Publishing, and Spirituality. Doron's background and 24 years of experience in meditation training, Meridian tapping (also known as E.F.T), Subliminal Messaging and other modalities has made him a much sought after expert in the self help and spirituality fields. His conversational writing style and his ability to take complex topics and make them easily accessible has gained him popularity in the genres that he writes for. He resides in New York City.

If you are interested in his other books on Switchwords, please take a look at the other kindle titles below:

Switchword Miracles Series:

Volume 1: Switchword Miracles

Volume 2: Switchword Subliminals

Volume 3: What You Resist, Persists

Volume 4: Get Sober with Switchwords And Meridian Tapping

This one: Volume 5: Switchwords And Your Chakras

Upcoming Title

Volume 6: **Switchwords : Advanced Techniques** . To be notified when this book comes out please feel free to go to http://www.switchwordmiracles.com and sign up to our newsletter. There are also podcasts, blogs and other information on Switchwords. Hope to see you there.

Doron can be reached at

mailto:doron@switchwordmiracle.com

If you are interested in seeing his Books on History Please go to

https://www.amazon.com/author/dmalon

Printed in Great Britain
by Amazon